NE

MANAGEMENT
DEVELOPMENT

SUPER S E R I E S

THIRD EDITION
Managing Activities

Leading Change

Published for
&NEBS Management   *by*

Pergamon
Flexible
Learning

Pergamon Flexible Learning
An imprint of Butterworth-Heinemann
Linacre House, Jordan Hill, Oxford OX2 8DP
225 Wildwood Avenue, Woburn, MA 01801-2041
A division of Reed Educational and Professional Publishing Ltd

℞ A member of the Reed Elsevier plc group

OXFORD   AUCKLAND   BOSTON
JOHANNESBURG   MELBOURNE   NEW DELHI

First published 1986
Second edition 1991
Third edition 1996
Reprinted 1998, 1999, 2000, 2001

© NEBS Management 1986, 1991, 1996

British Library Cataloguing in Publication Data
A catalogue record for this book is available from the British Library

ISBN 0 7506 3302 6

For information on all Butterworth-Heinemann publications
visit our website at www.bh.com

PLANT A TREE

BTCV
British Trust for
Conservation Volunteers

FOR EVERY TITLE THAT WE PUBLISH, BUTTERWORTH-HEINEMANN
WILL PAY FOR BTCV TO PLANT AND CARE FOR A TREE.

The views expressed in this work are those
of the authors and do not necessarily reflect
those of the National Examining Board for
Supervision and Management or of the publisher.

NEBS Management Project Manager: Diana Thomas
Author: Joe Johnson
Editor: Diana Thomas
Series Editor: Diana Thomas
Based on previous material by: Joe Johnson
Composition by Genesis Typesetting, Rochester, Kent
Printed and bound in Great Britain

Contents

Workbook introduction

Here are the workbook titles in each module which link with *Leading Change*, should you wish to extend your study to other Super Series workbooks. There is a brief description of each workbook in the User Guide.

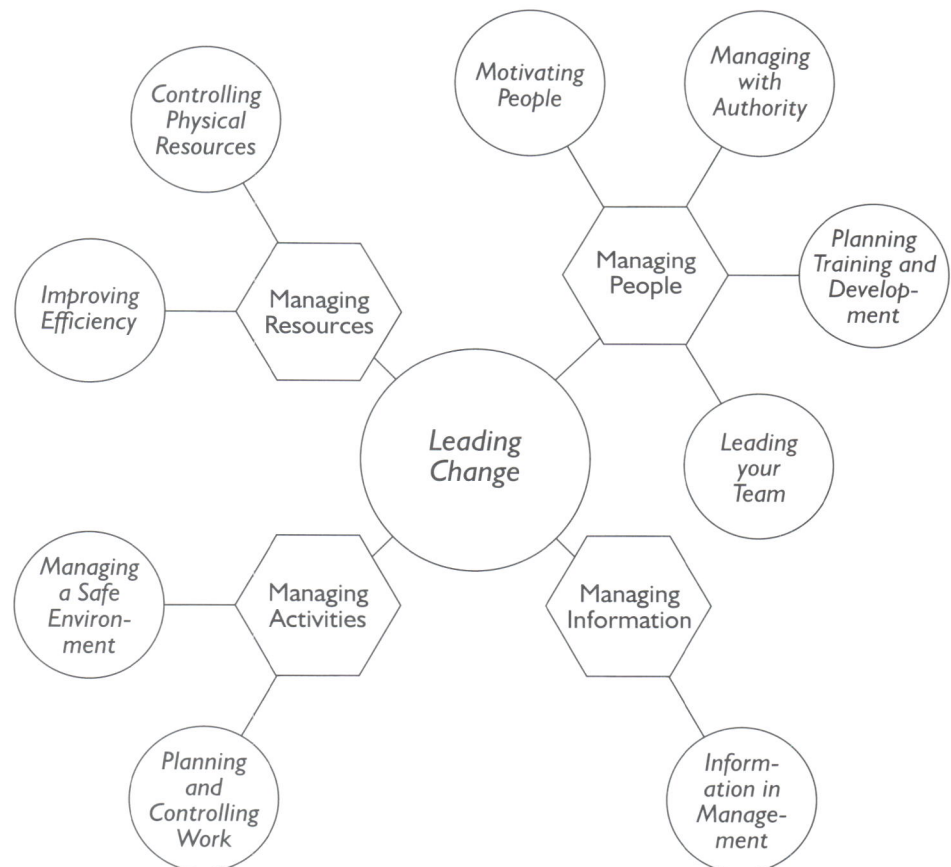

v

2 S/NVQ links

This workbook relates to the following elements:

A1.3 Make recommendations for improvements to work activities
C12.1 Plan the work of teams and individuals
C12.3 Provide feedback to teams and individuals on their work

It will also help you develop the following Personal Competences:

- building teams;
- focusing on results;
- thinking and taking decisions;
- influencing others.

3 Workbook objectives

Nothing is permanent but change.

This thought was expressed by Heraclitus, a Greek philosopher living around 500 BC. At the present time in our history, when the rate of change seems to be increasing, the truth behind the above statement is self-evident, particularly when applied to the world of work.

The days when employees did the same job, in the same way, for most of their working lives are long since gone. The working environment has seen many dramatic and far-reaching changes over the last forty years and it is difficult to imagine that 'the good old days' (if ever they existed) will return.

As we will discuss, change is not a single hurdle: a problem to be got out of the way before you get back to normal. Change goes on all the time. No organization and no team can afford to stand still; there's no room left for complacency. Yesterday's ways are for yesterday's people.

You, as a team leader, are likely to be involved both as an instigator of change, and as one who has to lead and inspire a team to implement the plans of others efficiently and productively.

This workbook will tell you about the forces behind change and the effects that it has on people's lives. You will learn how to steer round obstacles, overcome objections, and to adopt the most effective approach for leading your team. This will enable you, as a key player in your organization's hierarchy, to make a valuable and valued contribution to the implementation of planned changes.

We will investigate the nature of change, and examine some of the challenges and problems for the first line manager and the workteam which result from change. You will read that nearly all change brings both losses and gains. The skill of change management, therefore, is in minimising the effect of the drawbacks and maximising the benefits. Our discussions will include recommended methods and approaches to implementing change with minimum fuss and disruption.

3.1 Objectives

When you have completed this workbook you will be better able to:

- identify the forces behind change, and be aware of forthcoming changes;
- anticipate and recognize reactions to change, and overcome resistance to change;
- recognize the beneficial aspects of change, and adopt a positive attitude towards new thinking;
- manage the implementation of change, in particular by aiming to give your team a sense of ownership of the plans they are to implement, and so win their commitment.

4 Activity planner

The following Activities require some planning so you may want to look at these now.

- Activity 21 on page 32 which asks you to identify a major change at work in which you have already taken part and a second forthcoming major change;
- Activities 22, 23 and 34 on pages 34, 35 and 49 continue a consideration of the changes you have identified.

Portfolio of evidence

Some or all of these Activities may provide the basis of evidence for your S/NVQ portfolio. All portfolio activities and the Work-based assignment are sign posted with this icon.

The icon states the elements to which the portfolio activities and Work-based assignment relate.

The Work-based assignment (on page 60) suggests that you discuss with three workteam members or colleagues their experience of change. You might like to start thinking now about whom you should approach, and perhaps arrange a time to have a chat with them. This Assignment should be useful in helping to demonstrate your competence in:

- building teams;
- focusing on results;
- thinking and taking decisions.

Session A The nature of change

1 Introduction

Why can't they leave the game alone?

This recent headline, in the sports pages of a newspaper, headed an article which claimed that the rules of football had altered more in the past five years than in the previous hundred.

The people who change the rules of a game need to have good reasons for doing so. It's the same in any sphere of activity. When a procedure, or a principle, or a structure has stood the test of time, there has to be a sound justification for modifying or replacing it.

Major change generally comes about because of growth and development: new inventions open up new possibilities; experience points the way to a better approach; someone spots a fresh opportunity; old values are challenged because they no longer seem appropriate.

But minor change goes on all the time.

We begin this workbook by examining the way in which the world is constantly changing – the world of work in particular – and the underlying agents of change. Then we look at the way that some organizations are better adapted to change than others.

EXTENSION 1
In the book *Organizational Behaviour*, by Andrzej Huczynski and David Buchanan, another view of the forces of change is taken. External forces or triggers of change are listed as: 'Technology; Customers' tastes; Competitors' activities; Materials; Legislation; Social or cultural values; Changing economic circumstances.'

2 Forces for change

Changes come about as a result of three kinds of forces:

■ technological

   new technology and new ways of applying technology

■ social and legal

   changes brought about by the influence of people and of laws

■ economic

   changes brought about through pressures on costs and efficiency.

1

Activity I

Read these examples and say what you think helped to bring the changes about in each case.

- Caroline Quigley has been a clerk at the old-established firm of Terence Gratton Ltd for more than twenty years. Until five or six years ago, she would have described her job as 'mostly paperwork'. Then the company computerized nearly all clerical functions, and Caroline had to learn to work at a keyboard, and to produce results using a complex 'customized accounting package'. It was a difficult period of adjustment, but now she couldn't imagine going back to the old ways.

  However, as Caroline had discovered, it wasn't a simple question of learning a set of procedures and putting them into practice. The organization has been branching into new areas of business and its customer base is continuously changing. In addition, the software company that provided the computer package is regularly updating the system, and the equipment has already twice been upgraded.

  When she thinks about it, Caroline is surprised by how well she has coped with it all. Although she had been 'computer illiterate' just a few years ago, others in the office now look to her for expert help.

  _____

Were these changes to Caroline's job brought by:

Technology?
Social factors?
Economic factors?

Briefly explain the reasons for your selection.

  _____

  _____

- Polly Martin was 'spokesperson' for the UK arm of a company marketing a range of sportswear products. The company sourced many of its products in the Far East, and Polly was unhappy about the fact that the wages paid to employees in some of these 'sweat shops' in China and Burma were very low. Then several articles in the British press appeared, in which this state of affairs was drawn to the public's attention. Polly was called upon to justify the position of the company, and was asked by one interviewer if she believed in slave labour. Polly told her manager that she found it almost impossible to defend the company's policies; it wasn't enough to say 'If we didn't do it someone else would'. Eventually, the company was forced to reconsider its sourcing arrangements.

  _____

Was this change brought by:

Technology?
Social factors?
Economic factors?

Briefly explain the reasons for your selection.

_____

_____

■ Not many years ago, the historic dining clubs of London were 'exclusive' in more senses than one. Traditionally, they have been places where 'Gentlemen' meet: ladies were excluded, foreigners were frowned upon, and it was inconceivable that non-white members should be allowed. Now, here, as in may other sectors of society, the barriers are slowly coming down. Women are now welcomed in many clubs, and one famous establishment recently admitted its first black member, an event described as 'unthinkable twenty years ago'.

_____

Are these changes being brought by:

Technology?
Social factors?
Economic factors?

Briefly explain the reasons for your selection.

_____

_____

■ John Frederick's bookshop was the only one in the growing town of Busbury and brought him a steady but unspectacular income. Then a new shop opened in the town, belonging to a large chain of bookshops. John wasn't particularly worried at first, as he felt he could continue to compete. But the new shop started selling many titles at reduced prices, and offering further discounts to regular customers. In spite of his best efforts, within a short time John's shop was only doing half the trade it had before, and he went out of business.

_____

Was this change brought by:

Technology?
Social factors?
Economic factors?

Briefly explain the reasons for your selection.

_____

_____

See how far you agree with my assessment:

- In Caroline Quigley's case, there was certainly technology involved, as computerization only comes about through advances in technology. But the investment in technology was part of the company's efforts to stay efficient, and to keep up with a changing marketplace. Thus you might have said, reasonably enough, that the root cause of the changes was an economic one.
- Polly Martin, in the sportswear company, seems to have been influenced by social considerations, and her own conscience. Again, however, you could argue that, because the aim of any commercial company is to make a profit, any changes it made as a result of public pressure were to ensure that it could continue to sell its products. Both social and economic factors came into play here.
- There isn't much question that the new developments gradually being seen in many establishments in Britain are the result of changing social attitudes. Neither money nor technology seem to play any part.
- The forced closure of John Frederick's bookshop appears to have been brought about by competition, which is an economic force. There might have underlying social forces at work, too: perhaps part of the problem was that people in the town were buying fewer books.

Isolating one factor as the origin of change is not always easy. Economic, technological and social forces may all have an influence on decisions made in the workplace. Of course, in the world of work, financial considerations can never be ignored. Even when economics is not the direct cause of change, it nearly always influences the actions of those involved.

Changes come about because of technology, social and legal factors and, more often than not, economics.

3 Technology as a force for change

A great many changes which take place at work are driven by developments in technology. If we go back in history, the most fundamental change in working life in Britain came about as a result of the invention of machines such as the spinning jenny and the steam engine in the eighteenth century. Before this Industrial Revolution, most people worked on the land or in cottage industries. After that time there was a vast increase in the number of people toiling in factories and coalfields.

Now, again thanks partly to technology, we seem to be coming full circle, as many more of the population are working from home or in small businesses. The post-industrial revolution is with us: only about 20 per cent of workers in Britain are employed by industrial firms, and most coal mines have been closed.

But who can say whether this will still be the picture in twenty or thirty years' time?

Activity 2

4 mins

Apart from the obvious example of the computer, list some modern inventions that have changed or are in the process of changing the way people work. Jot down **two** or **three**.

_____

_____

_____

A recently announced material, made from wood pulp, is described as having the properties of 'making tough clothing soft' and 'weatherproofing without losing its softness', so that 'denim feels like cashmere'.

You might have mentioned:

- the car and the motorway;
- modern telecommunications, including the telephone, satellite links and fibre-optics;
- the aeroplane;
- high-speed trains;
- space technology;
- electricity and electronics;
- automation and industrial robots;
- agricultural machinery;
- modern fabrics;

or a hundred other inventions.

What is clear is that technology is changing all our lives and promises to alter them even more in the future.

Activity 3

3 mins

Perhaps you have given some thought to the future of the kind of work that you do and the way that it might be affected by advances in technology. Make a note of two ways in which you anticipate your working life may be changed within the next few years as a result of new technological applications.

_____

_____

_____

5

You might have written something like: 'The way things are going, we'll communicate with computers by thought transference next.' Anyone can speculate about what might happen in the future. What is more useful is to base your predictions on known facts. For example, if you use plastics, are you aware of developments in the chemical industry, where new kinds of plastics are being tested? Or if you work in building, you may have heard about new materials or processes, which may outdate existing practices. Most kinds of work are likely to change in the future as a result of new technology.

These advances can be expected to be generally beneficial, but they may cause headaches for those who are not prepared for them.

Wise managers make it their business to keep a close watch on changing events in their own industry, whatever the causes.

How can this be done? Some useful ways are:

- reading journals and newspapers;
- talking to suppliers' representatives;
- reading company newsletters and bulletins;
- attending management briefings;
- going on relevant courses;
- talking to colleagues in other parts of the organization, and in other organizations.

4 Social and legal factors

Changes brought about by social factors may be fleeting or permanent. In the clothing trade, all manufacturers and sellers have to respond to fashion. What has been popular in the past is no indicator of what people will buy in the future. Yet fashions return – the length of women's skirts alter from year to year, for instance: sometimes shorter, sometimes longer.

You may be in an industry or business which is subject to variations in demand patterns as tastes and fashions fluctuate. If so, you will be well used to having to adapt to market changes.

Public opinion is not always so fickle, however: other changes have more deep-rooted origins.

4.1 Public opinion

Activity 4

3 mins

Can you think of an example of how public opinion has altered over a period of time, so that attitudes, beliefs and standards held in the past look likely never to be acceptable again? If so, write it down.

_____

_____

_____

One such example is what can be called 'global awareness'. There is now wide acknowledgement that we cannot afford to ignore the effects that human activities have on the planet we inhabit. Much attention has been given to the facts that:

■ the earth does not have unlimited resources for humankind to exploit and destroy;
■ environmental phenomena such as global warming and the greenhouse effect are giving serious cause for concern.

Not even all scientists agree about many questions on the environment. But you don't have to be a 'green' to admit that there has been a significant change in public awareness of these issues.

Suppliers of goods or services cannot afford to ignore public opinion in this area. Customers demand 'environmentally friendly' goods and require that organizations take a responsible approach towards pollution. It is difficult to see how, in the future, people will go back to an uncaring attitude towards the environment.

One of many possible instances of change brought about by public awareness is that of the refrigeration industry. As you may know, a depletion of the ozone layer, high up in the atmosphere, has been discovered. This layer of ozone is what filters the sun's rays, and protects us from over-exposure to ultra-violet radiation; if the layer were to disappear completely we would all be dead. Its loss is blamed on substances produced by industrial processes. Chemicals called chlorofluorocarbons (CFCs), traditionally used in refrigerators among other things, have been identified as being partly to blame. It has been proved that CFCs react in the atmosphere with ultra-violet radiation to form chlorine, resulting in the ozone being converted to oxygen. Public opinion has forced governments and manufacturers to respond: there is a ban on the use of CFCs by the end of the century, and CFC-free refrigerators are already on sale.

Attitudes of humans towards one another is changing, too. In the world of work, equality of the sexes is gradually becoming a reality. You may argue that there's some way to go before women have the same opportunities as

7

men, but you cannot deny that public opinion on this subject has altered significantly over the past fifty years.

Another topic you may have mentioned is the increasing public concern over the exploitation of animals. This is beginning to have an effect not only on the way that products like cosmetics are tested, but on the way that animals are reared for food.

4.2 Information

You could say that the public is aware of these issues and of many others because of increased **information**. You may agree with other people that the real revolution taking place in society is being brought about by increased access to information of all kinds.

The amount of information we have undoubtedly affects our performance at work. In spite of phrases like 'the information explosion' – coined as a result of the seemingly unlimited capacity of the computer to store and print out data – it is still a more common problem at work to suffer from lack of information than a surfeit of it.

If you feel that you are lacking information, you share a problem with many other managers. It has been said that most decisions at work have to be made based upon insufficient knowledge.

A secondary problem is that the information we do get is not always the information we need, so we don't know what to do with it.

4.3 The law

The law affects employment in many ways. For example, it has brought about changes, generally for the better, in working practices. Less than 150 years ago a law was passed forbidding the employment of children under ten years of age in coal mines. At that time workers had virtually no rights. Today the working population is protected in a number of ways, through a series of Acts of Parliament.

This is one area of law – employee protection law.

Other kinds of laws which affect the workplace include:

- health and safety law;
- laws governing the conduct of unions;
- contract law;
- insurance law;
- consumer protection law;
- laws controlling the carriage of goods;
- company law, which deals with the registration of companies and the auditing of company finances.

5 Economic factors behind change

■ In 1943 an American patent lawyer named Chester Carlson invented a new process for copying documents. For six years he tried to sell his idea to all the big companies of the day, without success. The problem was that Carlson's invention was too revolutionary. No one could be sure that a market for it would exist.

Eventually he persuaded a small company called Haloid to take the risk. That company later became the Xerox Corporation and the success of the photocopier is legendary.

Should we blame the companies that turned down the idea for lack of foresight? Perhaps. We often read of companies failing to take advantage of opportunities, as in the case above. But many ventures do fail and many inventions are not very practical, for one reason or another.

The fact is that businesses continue to exist only if they make a profit – or at least don't make a loss.

Therefore a company cannot contemplate a new idea without considering its cost-effectiveness. To make changes – or to decide not to make them – on technical or social grounds alone is to put the company at risk.

Activity 5

3 mins

Most organizations are subject to economic pressures of many kinds. Some come from outside the company and some from inside.

Jot down **two** or **three** economic pressures to which an organization may have to react.

_____

_____

_____

_____

_____

You could have listed:

- the pressure of competition: to compete with their rivals, companies have to try to make their goods or services more attractive in some way, so as to retain or increase their share of the market;
- pressure from shareholders, who demand high profits and dividends;
- pressure from workers for higher wages, shorter working hours or better conditions;
- pressure from financial institutions, who lend the money organizations need for investment, but who demand interest and prompt payment.

We have noted that the origins of change may be technological, social or legal, economic or some combination of the three. Whatever the cause, it is part of the manager's job to be aware of developments in his or her own field of work.

6 Change and normality

Let us now look at the nature of change from some other viewpoints.

Activity 6

3 mins

Which of the following statements comes closest to describing your own work experience?

a Change is something unusual – a disruption to the everyday routine. When it occurs, we have to find ways of dealing with it. Provided we manage to get through the experience, we can get back to normality.
b Change is always with us. It may progress in a series of jumps, but we have to live with continuing change. Normality is whatever the situation is today. If we try to revert to yesterday's way of thinking, we are likely to get into difficulties.

Is (a) or (b) more realistic, in your view? Explain your reasoning, briefly.

_____

_____

_____

_____

_____

If someone at work thirty years ago were asked this question, the answer may well have been (a). People talked about 'having a steady job', and many jobs followed a predictable routine. Of course, changes did take place – organizations moved premises, people were promoted, new product lines were introduced and so on. But these could be identified as departures from an established pattern.

Perhaps you agree that these days, in all walks of life, in all trades and professions, it is very difficult to define normality. It has become 'normal' to expect regular announcements of:

■ mergers and takeovers

> **Nowadays, the only thing you can say with certainty about your job is that it will change!**

If we want to keep up with 'who owns whom' we must be keen students of the financial press. (Is your local electricity company now under French control? Or is it part of the same organization that delivers your water?)

■ businesses closing down or opening up

These result in many redundancies on the one hand or many new jobs on the other.

■ dramatic political changes, affecting millions of people

The past few years have seen the demise of the USSR and the fall of the Berlin wall, the growth of the European Union, the emergence of major new markets in the Pacific, and many other significant events. All such developments bring new opportunities and are likely to have an effect on the way that work organizations are run.

■ Technological advances

As we have already discussed, many of these promise (or threaten) to make us revise our ways of working.

Apart from these large-scale changes, we have to deal with local events, just as important to us. If every day were like the last, we would not get the chance to use our skills and to develop as individuals.

It doesn't seem to be helpful to try to identify what is normal, because

in a very real sense, change is the norm.

7 Features of change

Change is continuous: that is one of its features. Typically, and in work situations this seems to be especially true, change is also complex.

One aspect of this complexity is that most change has a good and a bad side. A change which is, on the face of things, entirely beneficial, will bring problems and drawbacks in its wake. And a planned event that seems to be

In summary, change is:

- continuous
- complex
- usually untried
- often difficult to manage.

hanging like a black cloud often turns out to have a silver lining. We will look at the beneficial and detrimental aspects of change later in the workbook.

Another consequence of complexity is that change is frequently difficult to manage. Perhaps you have been through the experience of having been made redundant, or of seeing colleagues 'released', leaving those left to cope with more work than they could handle. In Session C, on page 51, we will consider the special problems of redundancy.

A third feature of change is that it is, by definition, untried in a particular set of circumstances. No one, from the chief executive downwards, can describe with complete certainty how plans will turn out. That is why feedback is so important. This point will come up again on page 33 in Session C.

8 Adapting to change

The importance of responding to the forces of change has already been mentioned.

Here are **two examples** of companies changing their product lines.

Activity 7

4 mins

- The Brindley Manufacturing Company had been in the business of making and erecting garages for a number of years. Their new Marketing Manager, Derek Grimthorpe, recognized a market trend towards DIY products and worked with the company's designers to introduce a new range. Instead of selling a standard product, which was then put up on site by a trained team of erectors, the new range would allow customers effectively to design and put up their own garages. They could do this by selecting from a variety of components and slotting them together.

What effects might such a venture have on the way that the company operated its business?

For example, a new stock control system would probably be needed.

What other new ways of operating might it affect? Jot down your ideas briefly.

It is possible to visualize very significant effects on the company's business.

- New components would have to be manufactured and stored.
- A distribution network would have to be set up.
- The skilled teams of erectors might become redundant or have to be retrained.
- New selling methods may be required.

Activity 8

4 mins

- Rose's was originally a shipping firm. They developed lime juice to help prevent their sailors from getting scurvy through lack of fresh fruit. Their shipping business declined, but the lime juice was popular, so Rose's moved out of shipping altogether and into lime juice production.

The changes which took place at Rose's must have been fairly fundamental. In broad, general terms, what kind of changes would they have to make by starting to produce lime juice and cease the shipping business?

For instance, they would have had to employ people with different skills. Try to think of **two** suggestions.

You may have suggested that Rose's would have had to:

- utilize new technology – fruit presses and so on;
- find ways of distributing the lime juice and finding outlets for it;
- adapt to new ideas and methods.

Most importantly, they would have had to:

- **organize things differently**, because different sorts of activities would have to be co-ordinated.

In fact the whole **structure** of the company would have had to be changed.

8.1 Structure

The way a company organizes things is reflected in its structure – and vice versa. Some structures adapt to change more easily than others.

Activity 9

3 mins

Can you think of any kind of organization that operates in very stable conditions? Such an organization would have a consistent demand for its goods or services, would not need to worry about new technology or competition and could carry on in much the same way from year to year.

Spend just a few minutes thinking about this and see what you come up with.

_____

_____

_____

_____

_____

You may have found it difficult to think of such an organization. A funeral undertaker has a steady demand for its services, but even among undertakers there is competition. A few years ago one might have said that some of the major national institutions – the Inland Revenue for example – fall into this category. But this is no longer the case. The Inland Revenue, along with other major organizations, has undergone major changes as a result of demands for improved efficiency. They are certainly not untouched by technology.

In most businesses there is a great deal of compulsion to adapt. No business can afford to operate in the same way year in year out, without paying heed to new ideas, new technology, new social trends, new legal constraints and so on.

Another way of putting this is to say that

all organizations have to be flexible enough to respond to change quickly.

This means that the right decisions have to be made and then those decisions acted upon in as short a time as possible.

Activity 10

4 mins

Read the following accounts of two different companies and say which you think would adapt to change more quickly, and briefly why.

- In Company A:

  - decisions are made at the top;
  - everyone's job is precisely defined;
  - each level of staff is responsible for the work done by the level immediately below;
  - all instructions and information pass up and down through each level in the company;
  - procedures are 'written in stone', and suggestions for improvements are frowned upon.

  _____

- In Company B,

  - decision-making responsibility is handed down, rather than decisions;
  - job descriptions allow for personal development and changing conditions;
  - communications run both up and down and across the organization, and are more like two-way consultations than one-way commands;
  - people are encouraged to guide projects in the way that they believe they will work, rather than simply accepting orders from above;
  - training is given when and where it is needed, so that the right skills and knowledge are available.

  _____

  _____

  _____

  _____

You may well have argued that a bureaucratic firm like Company A might be able to implement changes more quickly. All that needs to happen is for management to issue an instruction for a change and the workforce carry it out.

However, **instigating change** is one thing; **making change work** is rather more difficult. To be implemented effectively, the change has to be accepted and 'owned' by the workforce. If employees see change as something imposed upon 'us' by 'them', they will find it much more difficult to be enthusiastic about it.

Ownership is the key to success in implementing change.

Those who feel they own something are much more likely to take care of it.

Many organizations are beginning to realize that ownership is an excellent motivator. Worker shares are becoming more common for that reason.

How can this feeling of ownership be engendered? How can you make your team believe that the proposed change is their property? The clues are there in the practices of our 'Company B'.

The successful organizations ensure that everyone:

- gets the chance to participate in realizing the change
- has the right information, knowledge and skills to handle the change.

Activity 11

(5 mins)

How well are you and your workteam able to adapt to change? Answer the following questions honestly by ticking the statements that best reflect your views.

I run my team based on my beliefs that:

a people only work hard when they have to – they need to be goaded into action ☐

b people work hard when they feel that they are working for their own benefit and what they do is meaningful to them ☐

c it is important for the team that I am in control of everything that goes on ☐

d it is best that all communications pass through formal channels; otherwise, there's chaos ☐

e everyone should be as fully informed as possible, because the most effective working relationships are based on a common understanding of needs ☐

f collaboration and informality work better than formality and withholding information ☐

g efficiency depends on everyone having a clearly defined job to do; that way, everyone knows what is expected and the work is more easily controlled ☐

h efficiency depends on flexible arrangements, so that workteams can adapt to changing requirements more easily; people should be able to move freely from activity to activity and work area to work area ☐

i people work best at simple, undemanding tasks, so it is best to break down jobs into small parts and cut out the need for people lower down the organization to make decisions ☐

j people work best if they are given complete and meaningful jobs to do; with the right opportunities for training, most people can cope with more difficult and demanding work, so it's best to keep variety and flexibility in jobs ☐

According to the experience of most successful organizations, the philosophy expressed by (b), (e), (f), (h) and (j) above are more likely to encourage adaptability to change than the attitude suggested by (a), (c), (d), (g) and (i).

So this is the main theme of our workbook. We have agreed that the successful organizations ensure that everyone has the right information, knowledge and skills to handle the change. We can also say that

Successful first line managers make sure their teams are enabled to cope with change. They do this by providing (fighting for if necessary) the required information, knowledge and skills.

This theme will be developed in Sessions B and C.

Self-assessment 1

10 mins

For questions 1 to 6, complete the sentences with a suitable word or words, chosen from the following list:

CHANGE	INDUSTRY	SKILL
CHANGING	INFORMATION	TECHNOLOGY
ECONOMICS	OWNERSHIP	
FLEXIBLE	PARTICIPATE	

1 Changes come about because of _____, social or legal factors and, more often than not, _____.

2 Wise managers make it their business to keep a close watch on _____ events in their own _____, whatever the causes.

3 In a very real sense, _____ *is* the norm.

4 All organizations have to be _____ enough to respond to change quickly.

5 _____ is the key to success in implementing change.

6 The successful organizations ensure that everyone:

a gets the chance to _____ in realizing the change

b has the right _____, knowledge and _____ to handle the change.

17

7 Say which **one** of the following statements is the **most** correct, and briefly explain the reason for your choice.

The companies which adapt to a changing environment most successfully will, amongst other things:

a have a stable hierarchy of management and will specify the jobs of workers precisely, so there's no room for doubt;

b give responsibility to lower management, who in turn will strictly control the way that changes are put into effect by the workforce;

c provide variety and flexibility in jobs and keep everyone informed of what's going on;

d make sure that what people do is meaningful to them but try not to confuse employees with information which isn't directly relevant to their jobs.

The most correct statement is _____ because:

_____

_____

_____

Answers to these questions can be found on page 69.

9 Summary

- Changes come about as a result of three kinds of forces: **technological**, **social and legal**, and **economic**.

- Technology has had an enormous influence on working life and is continuing to do so.

- New methods of collecting, analysing and distributing information are arguably resulting in more spectacular changes in the workplace than any other phenomenon.

- In business, **economic** considerations come first.

- It is naive to assume that change is a disruption of normality; in a very real sense, change **is** the norm.

- Change is continuous, complex, usually untried, and often difficult to manage.

- The way a company organizes things is reflected in its structure – and vice versa.

- All organizations have to be **flexible** enough to **respond to change quickly**.

Session B Attitudes to change

1 Introduction

Tempora mutantur, et nos mutamur in illis (Times change, and we change with them.) Anon.

Until around the early part of this century, people very decidedly 'knew their place' in society. People of stature – 'gentlemen' and 'ladies' – were easily recognized by the clothes they wore, their general demeanour and even their state of health. They could be distinguished at a glance from the 'hoi polloi'. Nowadays, although you could argue that a class system still exists in Britain, it is much less in evidence. Of course, there are still rich and poor people, but most other barriers are coming down. In practically every walk of life, ability counts for much more than who your parents are, or where you were educated.

We live in a changing world. The surprising thing is that people for the most part carry on from day to day, on the assumption that everything will continue in the way that it has done in the past. Human beings seem to need continuity, and in times of disruption, they yearn for 'normality'. As we have discussed, change is the only thing that has any real permanence, but this does not prevent us all from reacting against change.

In this session, we'll discuss reactions and resistance to change – why it exists and what its effects are.

The positive aspects to change will also be examined, and we will note that change brings new methods, new ideas, new possibilities.

Next, we'll focus in on the workteam: in what special ways are they likely to be affected by change?

2 Reactions to change

Activity 12

3 mins

- The workteam knew that their team leader, Piers Sloman, had been attending an important meeting with senior management. When he came back to the shop floor, several of his team looked at him expectantly.

  'I can't say anything except that there will be a lot of changes around here,' Piers said. 'You'll probably be told more next week.'

How do you think the team would react to a statement like that?

It wouldn't be surprising if the team members stopped work as soon as the leader's back was turned, to speculate about the possible changes. How could they be expected to concentrate with something like that hanging over their heads?

Unspecified changes will evoke strong emotions: often a mixture of anxiety, excitement and hope. Change is threatening – and at the same time offers new possibilities for the future.

Let's continue the story.

Activity 13

3 mins

- The following week Piers gathered the workteam together and made an announcement.

  'I can now reveal to you that the job we are now doing will cease as from this Friday. But there's no need for any of you to be concerned. You will all be reassigned to new duties. Of course, it will mean that many of you will have to be given training in new skills. Jean Winkler and I will be discussing your new jobs with you as soon as possible. Meanwhile, just relax and don't worry.'

Do you imagine that the team members will take Piers' last piece of advice? How do you think they will react now?

_____

_____

_____

_____

_____

I should think that, if they had difficulty concentrating on their work after Piers' earlier remarks, the team members may well now have trouble sleeping at night as well! What the manager has just said is that the whole of their working lives will change – and he expects them to relax!

Let's be honest: this kind of situation is not exactly unknown, is it? In many companies, drastic changes are planned without consulting the people most affected by them. And information is handed out piecemeal, so provoking the kind of negative reactions they would prefer to avoid.

Activity 14

5 mins

We've already discussed the fact that people need information. Well, Piers Sloman is apparently giving his team all the information he has. So, where is he going wrong? What should he have done differently? Think this over for a few minutes and then write down your ideas.

_____

_____

_____

_____

_____

In fact, Piers has not really given very much in the way of useful information. He has let it be known that drastic changes are planned which will affect the working lives of his team members. Without the details of just how each person will be affected, this is worse than knowing nothing.

I think it would have been better if Piers had said nothing – and preferably not have even disclosed at the start the fact that he was going to an important meeting.

Only when he had sat down with his manager (or whoever else was involved) and planned out the changes in detail, should he have made any announcement. This is not withholding information – it is preparing information so that it can be used effectively.

Of course, he might have to act quickly.

Activity 15

3 mins

Why might Piers have to work hard to get the details out quickly? What is the danger here?

_____

_____

_____

_____

_____

The danger is that the rumours of impending change may get out before all the details can be prepared. In many places of work there is a 'grapevine' which is capable of spreading information and misinformation very quickly. Should news of the proposals be 'leaked' Piers would be under great pressure, because the rumours would tend to have a similar effect to a premature announcement.

These kind of decisions are never easy: when to make announcements of change, what to say, who to tell first. They are not easy for any level of management. The important thing to bear in mind is that disturbing news is bound to upset people, so

it is important to think through the consequences of announcements about change.

3 Resistance to change

When faced with the prospect of change, people will often react by seeing it as a threat, especially when the implications of the change haven't been discussed with them.

For example, suppose a company announces a major change of policy and approach.

Activity 16

6 mins

Imagine that your organization has announced a new 'customer awareness' programme. The directors have made it clear that everyone will have to become more proactive in customer care. A series of seminars on the subject are to be held, which everyone will be expected to attend.

Your team normally have minimum contact with customers. Before the programme starts you talk to them about it to get their reactions. What sort of thing might they say? Write down two or three sentences of imagined overheard conversations.

_____

_____

_____

_____

_____

_____

A typical set of reactions might be:

- 'I hope this is not just another management gimmick.'
- 'This has nothing to do with us. We never see the customer.'
- 'I'm not a sales or marketing person. I'm not even very good at talking to people. How will I cope?'
- 'Will this mean that we will all have to start wearing smart suits?'
- 'Will we now be judged on how well we can chat people up? I'm a specialist, not a salesperson.'
- 'Just when I'd got this job taped up, they want to change everything. Why can't things go on as they did before? I thought it was all going well.'

Apprehensions and doubt about proposed changes are to be expected.

There is invariably an initial resistance to change. It's the kind of situation where first line managers need all their skills of tact and persuasion.

But managers themselves are often suspicious of the consequences of change, as the next case shows.

Activity 17

4 mins

■ In Threeways plc, a manager has been given the task of carrying out a feasibility study for reorganizing staff into new groupings, with the aim of making the firm more efficient. Before he works out the new proposals, he plans to talk to the department managers, then the first line managers, to find out how things are run at present.

What sort of response do you think the manager might get?

_____

_____

_____

You may agree with me that the manager may well encounter resistance and lack of co-operation. He may have difficulty in arranging interviews, because people are 'busy'. He may experience difficulties in finding out what he needs to know. He may be given incomplete or even misleading information.

Of course, if the case is typical, there will be those who will 'fall over themselves' to co-operate, because they see this proposed change as a chance to get a better job, or because they want to be seen as being co-operative.

Why do people resist change?

Activity 18

4 mins

Put yourself in the position of a manager whose team or department is being 'investigated' with a view to changing it. Why might you react in a negative way? What reasons might you have to fear change?

Spend a few minutes thinking about this and then write down your response briefly.

_____

_____

_____

_____

If you are like most people, you might well resent the interference of the investigation. But your reaction to the threat of change could be:

■ fear that you will lose your status or position;
■ worry that your career prospects will suffer;
■ anxiety about consequent loss of earnings.

Change may be seen as a threat to position, prospects or prosperity.

In addition, employees may feel:

■ anger that all the work they have done to build up the present system may now be thrown away;
■ that they aren't in control of their own destiny;
■ general uncertainty.

Resistance to change is a natural reaction, but, as we have discussed, most changes bring benefits as well as problems. We should now think about the beneficial elements of change.

4   The positive aspects of change

Change is the law of life. And those who look only to the past or the present are certain to miss the future.

John F. Kennedy, Frankfurt, West Germany
25 June 1963.

Change is an inevitable part of development, and it often brings hope and opportunity.

Activity 19

10 mins

How many positive aspects of change at work can you think of? For example, change can bring new interest to the job.

_____

_____

_____

_____

_____

_____

Would you agree with the following?

- Change can bring **new interest** to the job

How can there be progress without change?

Almost all jobs can become tedious or uninteresting after a time. A change can have the effect of reawakening enthusiasm and of stimulating a fresh appetite for the task.

- Change can open up new prospects for **career development**

Trying to make progress in your chosen career can sometimes feel the way a sailor feels, when trapped inshore in shallow water. No matter how much you desire to move on, there's nothing you can do about it – until the tide changes …

- Change can show a **new slant on things**

Doing the same job, in the same team, in the same way will make you start to believe there's no other way of doing it, after a while. It isn't until you break old habits that you see there are sides to the work you haven't contemplated. Change will provoke discussion, raise new questions, give new food for thought.

- Change can provide the opportunity to learn **new skills**

New technology, new systems, new people – these may all bring with them the prospect of adding new strings to your bow.

EXTENSION 2
Winning at Change, by George Blair & Sandy Meadows devotes a chapter to empowerment. As the book says of empowerment:

'Essentially, it involves sharing power throughout the organization. First line staff should have the authority to make most every day decisions, without reference further up the organisation.'

- Change can be a **challenge**

Instituting change is a new adventure. You're a pioneer, an explorer of the unknown. Can you stay cool in the face of fire?

- Change can provide an opportunity to **empower** the team: to give team members the scope and resources to gain more control over the work they do

If you're concerned about motivation, the problem could be that your team members don't feel involved enough in their assigned tasks. When change occurs, it could be the right time to loosen the reins a little – or a lot. We'll look at this again shortly.

In summary:

work is more rewarding for those who learn to identify the positive aspects of change.

These are some of the effects of change on the workteam. Let's investigate this aspect further.

5 Change and the workteam

Activity 20

5 mins

■ At the HiPrint works, there was a lot of discussion going on. It was a well-known fact that the company had been looking for new premises for some time. A few months previously, a lot of the staff had expressed concern that the firm would move away from the town – perhaps to one of those remote government development areas even – and that everyone would be given the choice of moving house or finding a new job. But nothing seemed to come of the idea and the workforce more or less forgot about it.

Now the rumour was going around that a new site had been found, five miles on the other side of town. As you can imagine, a lot of questions were being asked.

What do you think the main concerns of the workforce would be? Write down three or four questions that might be going through their minds.

_____

_____

_____

_____

_____

They would probably be asking questions like:

'Will any of us lose our jobs through the move – perhaps they'll try to recruit people in the local area?'

'How will I get to work? Is there a bus service? Will the company provide a company bus?'

'Will it mean that we'll have to get up earlier, or get home later?'

'Will we be paid compensation?'

'Will it be more – or less pleasant to work in?'

'If these are bigger premises, will there now be room for a canteen?'

In short, every member of the workforce will want to know

'How will the change affect me?'

27

Will it bring new problems and how will I deal with them? Will it perhaps bring new opportunities?

If you've ever been involved in a major change like moving premises, you will know something of the headaches it brings. For the team leader it can mean a hundred new problems, often compounded by the fact that management insist on minimum work being lost during the move.

For the team member, the worries are often more personal. The greatest fear in any upheaval is of job loss. After that, the concern will be over money, disturbance, intrusion and inconvenience. These anxieties are in addition to the unease felt about changes related to the job itself, which we've already discussed. The effects of all these cares may be to cause:

> A team leader needs to watch out for the signs of reaction against imagined threats behind change.

- emotional outbursts
- unreasonable and unreasoning behaviour
- lowering of work performance
- sickness or other absence
- argument and other conflict.

Once all the uncertainty has been resolved, most of the worries disappear and the mood changes – even before the change takes place.

It isn't change that creates the anxiety so much as uncertainty about change.

5.1 The effort of change

In the next session, we will go into the management of the change process in some depth. Before moving on, however, it is worth saying a word about the demands made upon teams and individuals when a major change takes place.

To get a large project, like moving premises, completed, the pace of work may have to be stepped up. While the project is proceeding, people who are thoroughly involved will be kept going by their interest and the desire to get the job finished.

After a sustained effort, however, people often feel flat and tired. The end of the project may come as something of an anticlimax. A good manager will recognize this fact. Time is needed to recover: nobody can work at an intense level for long without a period of recuperation.

In addition, you might like to think about the way that you acknowledge and reward the team for their exertions. Different teams celebrate in different ways. Some take a night out together; others are happy to be allowed time for 'pet' projects. You could send a letter of thanks, addressed either to the team as a whole, or to each person individually. It is very important to show appreciation for an endeavour above and beyond the call of normal duty.

A direct reward, in terms of extra pay or promotion, is not often possible. But frequently change brings new possibilities for personal development. How will you reward your team?

Self-assessment 2

10 mins

1   Fill in the words in the grid by solving the clues.

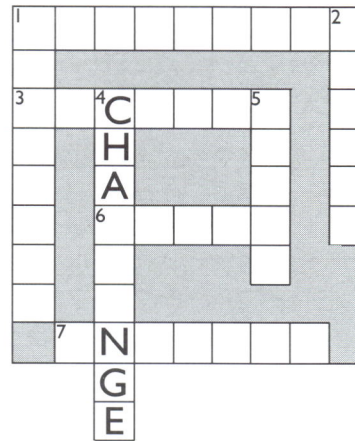

1 down and 1 across:	Change may be seen to be a threat to _____, _____ and prosperity. (8 and 9 letters)
6 across and 2 down:	Change can provide the opportunity to _____ new _____. (5 and 6 letters)
3 across:	Something we all seek. (7 letters)
4 down:	One of the positive aspects of change is that it can provide a new _____. (9 letters)
5 down:	Change can show a new _____ on things. (5 letters)
7 across:	It isn't change that creates the _____ so much as uncertainty about change. (7 letters)

For questions 2 to 5 pick the **one** word or phrase which is the **most** suitable, in each case:

2   Resistance to change is INAPPROPRIATE / DESIRABLE / NORMAL.

3   Emotional outbursts are often triggered by CHANGE / UNCERTAINTY ABOUT CHANGE / ARGUMENT AND CONFLICT.

4   One of the positive aspects of change is that it CAUSES RUMOURS / CAN PROVIDE A NEW CHALLENGE / PROVIDES INFORMATION.

5   Work is more rewarding for those who learn to identify the SKILLS OF MANAGEMENT / LEVEL OF COMPETENCE REQUIRED FOR THE JOB / POSITIVE ASPECTS OF CHANGE.

Answers to these questions can be found on page 70.

6 Summary

- It is important to think through the consequences of announcements about change.

- Change may be seen as a threat to **position**, **prospects** or **prosperity**.

- Change can:
    - bring **new interest** to the job;
    - open up new prospects for **career development**;
    - show a **new slant on things**;
    - provide the opportunity to learn **new skills**;
    - be a **challenge**;
    - provide an opportunity to **empower** the team:

- Work is more rewarding for those who learn to identify the positive aspects of change.

- The first question that comes into the minds of most people is: 'How will the change affect me?'

- When it comes to the workteam, it isn't **change** that creates the anxiety, so much as **uncertainty about change**.

Session C Managing change

1 Introduction

'Plus ça change, plus c'est la même chose.' (The more things change, the more they are the same.) Alphonse Karr, *Les Guêpes*.

There are really two kinds of change. One is the gradual variation that takes place over a period of time – perhaps we should call this unplanned change. Managing this kind of change in the workplace means monitoring results against fixed aims and objectives, to make sure that any movement taking place is in the right direction.

What we will be more concerned with in this session is deliberate, organized change: in other words, planned change. Planning is the key to controlling change, as we will discuss in this final session of the workbook.

First, though, we need to think about the team leader's role in change – that means you! This can be said to be the central topic of our subject. We'll discuss many aspects of the question: 'Just what is the team leader expected to do when changes are planned?'

Our next major topic is the techniques and skills involved in overcoming resistance to change. This is an attempt to resolve the problem posed in Session B.

Then we examine the planning process – what it consists of. This involves identifying what the key factors in a situation are.

Later in the session, a special word or two is given to the problems of the aftermath of redundancy.

Lastly, this session explains the importance of getting the atmosphere right – **before** changes are planned.

Portfolio of evidence C12.1

Activity 21

15 mins

This Activity may provide the basis of appropriate evidence for your S/NVQ portfolio. If you are intending to take this course of action, it might be better to write your answers on separate sheets of paper.

Before we start this session, think about your own work situation, and if possible identify **two** fairly major changes, one which you have already experienced, and one which you expect could happen in the near future.

In each case, briefly describe the change.

You will need your answer to Activity 21(a) for Activity 23.

a What was the event that has already taken place? What contribution did you and your team make to it?

_____

_____

_____

_____

_____

_____

_____

_____

_____

_____

b What is the change that you expect to be involved in shortly? Explain how you and your team plan to play your part in its implementation.

_____

_____

_____

_____

_____

_____

_____

_____

_____

_____

2 Change and the team leader

The title of this workbook is *Leading Change*. So far, we have placed a lot of emphasis on the forces for change, the nature of change and attitudes to change. Now it is time to turn our attention to the 'leading' aspects.

Major changes at work do not simply happen; they are made to work by people. The job of managers is to give the lead. All teams need to be led. This does not mean that people have to be told exactly what to do and when and how to do it. The primary skill of leading and managing is to find ways of gaining:

- influence
- trust and respect
- voluntary co-operation
- commitment to the task.

Team leaders are very often put under pressure by changes before anyone else, and are expected to act as the focal point for activities. Higher management may make most of the plans, and eventually the workforce feel their effect, but more often than not it is the team leader who has to turn plans into reality. The team leader's role may well encompass:

The points listed on the next couple of pages summarize the team leader's role in instigating and implementing change. The planning aspects will be covered later, starting on page 44.

- instigating change

    In many organizations, plans for change will be initiated by the higher levels of management. However, this need not always be the case. Why not take the lead yourself, when you see a need or an opportunity for change? You may need permission to put the change into effect, but your idea and enterprise may stand you in good stead. Your team, too, should be encouraged to put forward suggestions for improvements to processes, products and procedures.

- being aware of potential changes

    This includes the points we have already discussed in Session A: as a good manager, you have to make it your business to know what is going on in your industry, and in your organization.

- calculating costs

    You may simply be presented with a budget to manage. Alternatively, you may be asked to estimate costs of particular actions or processes.

- determining feasibility

    You and your fellow team leaders are often in the best position to know whether a proposal will work, or is achievable within a certain timescale or cost limit.

- feeding information back

    Your experience and your team may be key to the project, and you will be expected to contribute information to support the decisions made by your line manager and others.

Activity 22

10 mins

This Activity may provide the basis of appropriate evidence for your S/NVQ portfolio. If you are intending to take this course of action, it might be better to write your answers on separate sheets of paper.

If you haven't already mentioned feedback in your response to Activity 21(a), describe an occasion in the past when you gave feedback to your team which resulted in a modification to a planned change.

_____

_____

_____

_____

_____

_____

_____

_____

_____

Other elements in the team leader's role for change may include:

- working out a strategy for deployment of staff

  Staff deployment is usually part of the team leader's day-to-day job. Where substantial changes are underway, this aspect of the work can become more difficult than usual.

- deciding the best way to keep the team informed

  We looked at some aspects of this question in Session A (in the feedback to Activity 10 on page 15), and in Session B, starting on page 19. We will look at it again in this session.

- 'selling' the idea of the change to the team

  To sell something, whether it be a product, a process or an idea, it is necessary to persuade potential buyers that they will benefit from the exchange. In this case, the workteam will pay you in their commitment to the project.

- empowering the workteam to cope with the change

  It is not enough to sell the idea. You must empower your workteam to manage things in their own way. More and more, organizations are realizing that the old

EXTENSION 2
As the book *Winning at Change*, by George Blair & Sandy Meadows says:

'A key precondition for real empowerment is trust. Managers need to trust their staff so that they can learn from their mistakes without feeling threatened.'

ways of managing by telling people what to do and how to do it are no longer appropriate. As competition gets more fierce, greater commitment is needed from staff at all levels. The only sure way to achieve this is by allowing increased levels of freedom for people to organize their own work – to hand over control of tasks to those who have to accomplish them.

This is a courageous step: to hand over more authority to your team, and to watch them learn from their mistakes; it cannot be taken lightly. If and when you do it, the workteam will certainly depend on your full trust and support.

You will also have to provide them beforehand with the practical resources and training they need.

Portfolio of evidence A1.3

Activity 23

10 mins

This Activity may provide the basis of appropriate evidence for your S/NVQ portfolio. If you are intending to take this course of action, it might be better to write your answers on separate sheets of paper.

For the project that you listed in Activity 21 (a), describe the recommendations you made, and the steps you took, to provide the workteam with the necessary resources, (perhaps) including training.

_____

_____

_____

_____

_____

Continuing with our discussion of the team leader's role, we should include:

■ providing your team with the feeling of ownership of the change

Once you have sold the idea of the change, you can complete the deal by handing over ownership. The gain to you is the fact that owners tend to treat their possessions well. Your team must be made to feel they are:

■ not being kept in the dark;
■ not simply looking on from the sidelines;
■ not just helping implement the plans of management;

but controlling the action themselves. If you can manage to do this, they will become enthusiastic about the change, and promote it to others.

■ planning the logistics

By logistics, we mean managing the materials flow through your part of the organization. Depending on the work you do, materials may range from heavy goods to information.

■ coping with keeping things running during the change

This may be your greatest challenge.

This list summarizes the overall role of the team leader. We will get down to more specific lists of planning actions shortly.

Above all, the team leader is a facilitator for change. This means taking a suitable approach.

2.1 Adopting the right approach

Activity 24
3 mins

Suppose you are told, as a team leader, that there is to be a new paperwork system covering your team's work. The only thing you've heard about the new system is that it seems complicated, although you assume that it does have some advantages. How would you react, do you think?

_____

_____

_____

You might react by

■ questioning why a new system is needed, because the old one seems perfectly adequate;
■ groaning inwardly, knowing how hard it is to get people to use a new system – 'Not more work?!'
■ reserving judgement, until you've learned how the new system works and what advantages it offers;
■ wondering how these bureaucrats have time to invent paperwork systems when you're so busy.

The chances are that you will have mixed reactions, but you may decide to respond by being diplomatic and giving your full co-operation. You know that, as a team leader, you are expected to make things work, even if you have misgivings about them.

Activity 25

Because you're human, your normal reaction is to tend to resist change. But you are also a team leader, and an intelligent, responsible member of the organization.

When presented with proposals for change, how do you think you should react? Write down **two** positive, responsible ways to respond.

_____

_____

_____

_____

_____

_____

_____

There's no point in being negative, is there? After all, if you greet the proposals with scepticism and resentment, what can you expect from your workteam? The only sensible approach is to be open-minded and positive. You could have suggested:

> **The first line manager, perhaps more than any other level of management, is required to make the best of any given situation.**

■ forgetting vested interests

You may feel that the time and energy you've spent on the old system will now be wasted, but this shouldn't prevent you looking seriously at the new scheme.

■ setting aside your prejudices

We all have our opinions and preferences, but know that we ought not to let them cloud our judgement. (Nevertheless, if you have ideas of your own – perhaps you can see a better way of doing things – you might reasonably request an opportunity to present them.)

■ learning more about the new system

Any new scheme must have its merits; the more you understand it, the easier it will be to work with it.

■ using your knowledge to help the workteam

Because you recognize your own resistance to change, you can help overcome it in others.

2.2 Change fatigue

All that being said, it has to be acknowledged that the human reaction to change may sometimes be influenced by what might be called 'change fatigue'. In some places of work, change may seem to be instigated for its own sake, and without any seeming overall plan or objectives. If change after change takes place, people will naturally be reluctant to co-operate with the latest project, as they wonder when it will be supplanted by another one.

If this is happening, it must somehow be brought to management's attention.

But let's go back a stage. We are discussing a team leader's reactions – the way he or she may feel and the sensible way to respond. This all assumes that the team leader hasn't been consulted about the plans for change.

Activity 26

3 mins

What might be a better way for management to approach the idea of change, so far as their team leaders are concerned?

_____

_____

_____

_____

_____

I hope you agree that change should be the concern of the team leader at the earliest possible stage. Certainly this should be the case when team leaders are expected to put the change into effect.

The more involved team leaders are, the more support they can give.

Now we should turn our attention again to a problem discussed in Session B: the reaction to change.

3 Managing resistance to change

EXTENSION 1
Organizational Behaviour by Andrzej Huczynski and David Buchanan has a good chapter on organizational change. In it you will find a list of twelve rules for managing resistance to change.

We have seen that resistance to change is normal, and that its causes are:

- a perceived threat to position, prosperity or prospects;
- the natural inclination to hang on to what you know, rather than embrace something that is unfamiliar;
- uncertainty.

Activity 27

3 mins

- Two team leaders were discussing a new shift rota, that was being imposed on their teams without much consultation.

  Rashid was concerned about the reactions of some of his team to the proposals: 'I'm afraid that some of them will simply down tools. It really hasn't done a lot for morale.'

  Paul was more optimistic: 'I know things seem pretty bad at the moment. But give them another two weeks to get used to the idea. Things will settle down.'

In your experience, do you think that time tends to help people overcome resistance to change, as a general rule? Write down any views you have on the subject.

_____

_____

_____

_____

My opinion is that time certainly can have a kind of 'healing effect' to bruised feelings and the shock that a change can bring. However, I would qualify that by saying that time does not always eliminate resistance. Although people need time to get used to new ideas, they won't necessarily learn to accept and like them. The initial emotional response may fade, but a more considered and organized opposition to the change may appear.

It simply isn't enough for the team leader to sit back and 'wait for things to calm down'. A change has to be planned for and positive action taken to try to overcome resistance.

We've already discussed the idea that **empowerment** and **ownership** are the keys to success in implementing change. In particular, successful organizations ensure that everyone not only gets the chance to participate in realizing the change, but also has the right information, knowledge and skills to handle the change.

There's one more constituent needed for the recipe for successful change implementation: **enthusiasm**.

The three main ingredients can therefore be remembered by the letters PIE.

When planning a successful change, remember the PIE recipe:

- Participation
- Information
- Enthusiasm

3.1 Participation

Activity 28

5 mins

Suppose your team has been assigned some new equipment, to help you do your job more efficiently. The equipment is due to arrive in a month's time. Your main concern is that the team members will have to change their ways of working, learn how to use the equipment and yet continue being a productive unit during the period of change-over.

You decide that your first priority is to get everyone in the team thinking in a positive way about the change.

How would you approach this task? Jot down your thoughts briefly.

_____

_____

_____

_____

One approach is to describe the equipment to the team and point out that it is designed to make the job easier. This should certainly help to overcome any scepticism – people are obviously much happier to accept a change if they see it as helping to lessen their workload.

However, the worth of the equipment has yet to be proven. Meanwhile it may be seen as just another problem. For this reason, I would invite the team to participate in planning for the change. If people are involved in solving a mutual problem, they tend to concentrate on helping each other, rather than worrying about the effects on them personally.

How you go about this will depend on you and your team. You might feel it best to start by holding a general discussion, with you standing at a blackboard or flip-chart, writing down the points as they arise. The starting point could be: 'This is the new equipment. It looks like it could be useful to us. What we have to decide is how to get the most from it without letting it disrupt our normal work. I need your ideas. In fact, I will need you to organize the whole business.'

Or you might involve more senior members of the team first, perhaps putting the problem as 'How do we get these youngsters to cope with the new equipment?'

You know your team best, and what they are capable of, so there is no single approach that will work in all circumstances. One thing is certain, however:

Where change is concerned, participation is the best antidote to resistance.

3.2 Information

As we've discussed, one of the main causes of negative and emotional reactions against change is uncertainty.

The best cure for the anguish of uncertainty is information.

Projected changes provoke questions. If the questions go unanswered, they become problems; and the problems, real or imagined, will undermine the effectiveness of the plans.

Activity 29

Suppose you are in charge of the day-to-day running of a branch of a Building Society. The management have found new premises in the town and you are made responsible for planning and organizing the move. You are determined to keep your team fully informed, so as to avoid problems arising from uncertainty.

What actions could you take so as to do this effectively? Think about this for a few minutes, then write down at **least** three things that you might do.

_____

_____

_____

_____

_____

Some ways of approaching this situation, of keeping the team informed during a move, would be to:

> **Management by secrecy just doesn't work.**

- show them the new premises, collectively and/or individually: where they will work, the facilities available and so on;
- hold a meeting in which you announce details of the move, followed by a discussion session in which you do your best to answer any questions that arise;
- extend an invitation to all members of the team to discuss privately any particular problems they foresee, so you can try to overcome them together and allay any fears;
- make it clear to each person what part they have to play during the change-over, including what they should tell customers and so on.

Information is the best medicine for uncertainty.

3.3 Enthusiasm

It almost goes without saying that the team leader has to try to inspire enthusiasm, because enthusiasm helps smooth out the snags.

If the team members see that their leader is lukewarm and half-hearted about the proposals for change, they will tend to act in the same way.

Instigators of change who show fire and fervour are likely to carry the team along with them.

Activity 30

2 mins

Do you agree with this? Can you say why?

_____

_____

_____

I think it's true because

enthusiasm is infectious.

3.4 The down side

But what if you have misgivings about the proposed changes? It's hard to be enthusiastic if you don't agree with the changes you've been told to implement, or the way they are to be implemented.

Activity 31

5 mins

Let's imagine a situation where your company announces a new bonus scheme to replace an earlier one. You, along with other team leaders, are told about this and instructed to pass on details to your team. You first of all sit down and work out that, whereas most other teams will benefit from the new scheme, your team will actually be worse off than before.

What can you do? How can you go along to your team and enthusiastically announce the scheme knowing that all your group will be out of pocket? Think about how **you** would handle a situation like this.

Would you:

- pretend to your team that there really is no difference between the two schemes? ☐

- blame it all on management and say that it isn't your fault? ☐

- ask for an urgent discussion with your manager to point out the problem and ask for some changes to the scheme? ☐

- go to your manager and say that it's up to him or her to tell the team, as you don't want to be the unpopular one? ☐

- take some other action, namely:

_____

_____

_____

Well, your options may be limited, but at least you have to explore them all. What you **can't** do is to go along to the team and say something like: 'Management have really done it to us this time!' You can't do this because it will simply make team morale sink to rock bottom and create a rift in the company which may be hard to repair. Team leaders have to represent the workteam appropriately to management, and management properly to the team, or nothing they try to achieve will work well.

Also, there's no point in pretending that there isn't a problem. People are very quick to realize the fact that their income has been reduced, and then you would either look foolish or dishonest – or both.

> The question is always: 'How can I move forward in a positive way from the position I find myself in?'

Your best option in this case may be to request an urgent discussion of the matter with your manager, in which you point out the negative effects of the change, and perhaps ask whether your team can be compensated for their losses in some way. You might even propose an alternative scheme or a modification to the proposals. After all, the idea of bonus schemes is to provide an incentive to work harder. It isn't in the company's interests for them to have the opposite effect.

There are other kinds of situations where you may not agree with the changes proposed, yet accept the fact that they are inevitable. A company which is losing money may have to make some personnel redundant, for instance, or even close a part of its operation. These changes are always hard to face, and enthusiasm doesn't come into it. The best you can do is to try to soften the blow as much as the circumstances allow.

Once you have explored every aspect of change proposals with which you disagree, and have done all you can to put forward your and your team's point of view, then all that is left is to

be as positive and open-minded as you can.

4 Planning for change

As with so many management activities

getting the planning right is more than half the battle.

Activity 32

4 mins

Imagine you are a manager, running a team of people in a warehouse. The company you work for decides to reorganize its operation and as a result another group would be amalgamated with yours. This means that you would now be running two teams in warehouses a mile or so apart.

Imagine now that you are asked by your manager to draw up a draft plan for the change.

Without worrying about the details at this stage, what is the one thing you must do first?

_____

_____

_____

_____

_____

People set about planning in different ways. Your method of approach would be influenced by your background and the sort of change you are involved in.

In general, the process of planning consists of:

■ deciding what you want to achieve and by when – the objectives of the plan;
■ identifying the key factors in the situation;
■ making a list of actions to be taken.

4.1   The objectives of the plan

The importance of getting the objectives clear before the start can never be over-emphasized. Until and unless you know exactly want you have to achieve, it is improbable that you will be successful in achieving it. Writing down your objectives clearly at the start of a project is always time well spent. At the outset you may only be able to sketch out an outline of your aims, which can be refined and added to at a later stage.

These objectives are best agreed with the people involved, including your team, wherever possible.

Activity 33

In the case mentioned in the last Activity you had to imagine a situation in which you were asked to draw up a draft plan. Would it be appropriate to discuss your ideas about this with the team before you have talked them through with your manager?

_____

_____

The answer to this question depends on you, your team and the circumstances. You may feel that it would be unwise to draw the team into the discussions until you and your manager have a firm strategy. If the team members are to be affected by the plan, it probably won't be a good idea to talk to them about it if there is a chance that the plan will fall through. You have to balance this consideration with the general rule of trying to involve the team at the earliest possible stage. You must be the judge.

Use the following list as a guide when setting out the objectives of your own planned change.

Action points for objectives

> This is the first of two lists which you will need to refer to when you tackle Activity 34.

■ What is the point of the change – what problem does it solve?

Is the change necessary and/or desirable? Are you convinced of the value of the proposals? If not, who should you talk to about it? (Who will sell the plans to you?)

■ What are the objectives of the proposed change as defined by management?

Ideally, if management have instigated the change, it will be well-defined. If not, can you request that it is better defined, or can you define it?

■ How do these objectives need to be modified to meet local requirements?

The overall proposals may not take account of problems or other circumstances in your area.

■ Which teams, sections and departments are involved in the change?

Should you be discussing the proposals with other groups, to ensure a smooth operation? If not, how can you be sure that problems won't appear at the points of interface between you?

■ What are the constraints?

Constraints may include the financial limits, resources, etc.

■ What is the proposed timescale?

Is this timescale reasonable? Is it feasible? If you think it can't be done, how will you convince your team that it can?

■ Which people and what resources are available to assist you in planning the change?

The planning stage itself may be constrained by available resources. But you still have to make it work!

■ Which people and what resources are available to assist in implementing the change?

At the implementation stage, a great deal of concentrated and co-ordinated effort may be required.

■ How will normal working life be affected during the change?

Planning change during normal operations is the norm rather than the exception. Don't underestimate the potential disruption and chaos.

4.2 Identifying the key factors in the situation

Having determined what is to be achieved, a list can be made of all the aspects which will need further thought, and the consequences of any proposed actions. In short: you have to think the thing through.

Use the following list of key factors as a guide for your own change planning process.

Key factors

> This is the second of the two lists which you will need to refer to when you reach Activity 34.

■ Changes in your way of working

Will you have to delegate more? Will you have to operate from a different base? Will you have more informal contact with the team, or more formal meetings?

■ Changes in the team's way of working

More subgroups? New procedures? A different structure?

■ Training requirements

What new skills must be learned? How will they be acquired? Formal or informal training?

- **Changes in communication procedures**

  Easier communications – or more difficult? Between team members, between you and the team, between this team and other people?

- **The organization structure that would support the new arrangements**

  Should you appoint senior team members to new positions of authority? What about your position?

- **How each individual will be affected**

  The safest way is to make a list and consider each team member individually.

- **Which other groups will be affected**

  Who will be affected? How will they be affected? What should you do to bring them into the picture?

- **How information about the change will be issued**

  When should you begin consulting? Who should be consulted? Who needs to know? How will you present the news?

- **The likely reactions and sources of resistance to the change**

  If you know the team well, you should be able to anticipate reactions to a large extent.

- **Perhaps an estimate of costs**

  This point was mentioned on page 46.

- **The timetable for introducing the change**

  Should you identify milestones – defined points which signify specifically when certain achievements should have been made – on the way to the overall objectives?

Although they will vary in importance according to circumstances, all the above factors should be given consideration.

For instance, in the example given of amalgamating two teams, items such as costs and training may initially be dismissed as being inapplicable. But the team leader's change of responsibility will have many repercussions. Because nobody can be in two places at once, it might be necessary to appoint two new leaders, each reporting to the manager. Does this mean supervisory training? If so, how will the costs be met?

4.3 Making a list of actions to be taken

Once the ramifications of the change have been thought through, you next have to decide – in detail – what actions you plan to take. This can be called the preparation stage. You will often have to go back to the previous stage in doing this, because, as you plan the actions to take, you will think of new angles to consider.

Again, chances of success are increased if the team are brought into this process – assuming it is appropriate to do so.

Preparation will include scheduling the resources and the people. A complicated change may require you to draw up schedules and charts detailing the resources needed at each stage. In any case you will have limited resources, especially if you are trying to continue a day-to-day operation while the change is taking place.

Portfolio of evidence C12.1

Activity 34

15 mins

This Activity may provide the basis of appropriate evidence for your S/NVQ portfolio. If you are intending to take this course of action, it might be better to write your answers on separate sheets of paper.

For the change you identified and described in Activity 21, you should now plan your approach.

On separate sheets of paper, go through the points in the two lists above: 'Action points for objectives' (on page 46) and 'Key factors' (on page 47). Select all those that could possibly apply in your situation. Add any other points you think of.

EXTENSION 3
This book provides some helpful advice on implementing change, and case studies which you could compare with your own experience.

Your work on this Activity will provide you with a structured approach to change implementation. You could develop this further by writing down your planned actions in detail against each point on your lists. A detailed plan of action like this is good preparation for future changes. It would be even better if you document how you use the plan to implement and monitor the change process.

5 The process of change

The process of change involves changing people.

Activity 35

3 mins

Consider a situation in which a small chain of shops has, until recently, been a newsagents and general stores. Now, following a change in the law, the management have the opportunity to set up Post Office facilities in the shops.

For the local branch managers, this is a big development. Jot down **two** ways in which they will be affected.

_____

_____

_____

Your jottings may have included some of the following points:

- learning about running a Post Office;
- reorganizing the shop;
- reassigning staff;
- learning about the detailed clerical operations involved;
- setting up secure counters and having safes installed;
- liaising with the Post Office sorting office staff.

These kind of changes in the way people think and act can be put into **three** categories:

- changes of attitude
- changes of skill
- changes of knowledge.

5.1 Unfreezing and refreezing

The stage of preparing people for change is often called **unfreezing**.

This means reducing resistance towards change and creating a climate in which change can more easily take place. Another way of putting it is saying that unfreezing 'warms people up' to the idea of change.

Refreezing occurs once the change has taken place.

50

It takes time for people to become accustomed to new skills, new ways of working and the application of new knowledge. You can't expect the same level of performance straight away. It should also be remembered that it will take time to build up to earlier levels of confidence, because confidence only grows as competence increases.

Activity 36

4 mins

The process of change is not complete until the team is working to at least its former efficiency. Which of the following would you include in your approach, assuming you want to complete the implementation of a change as effectively as possible? Tick more than one box if you wish.

a Being receptive to feedback, as you want to get the team involved. ☐

b Not taking too much notice of comments, on the grounds that all changes are bound to bring a few grumbles. ☐

c Being rather dogmatic about the way that the plan is put into effect as you want to be seen 'leading from the front'. ☐

d Being prepared to revise your plans in the light of experience and new knowledge. ☐

e Seeking the opinions of the workteam at all stages. ☐

I would choose (a), (d) and (e) as the most appropriate and effective way to behave. Plans are seldom put into effect without modification, because it is very difficult for planners to foresee all the consequences of the change. During the refreezing stage, snags and problems will inevitably arise. The sensible team leader will watch out for these, listen to the comments of the team members and be prepared to make adjustments.

Be prepared to change your plans for change.

6 Life after redundancies

We hear a lot about the trauma suffered by people who have been made redundant. This is understandable. Security of employment hardly exists any more, and we are naturally sympathetic when someone suddenly finds him- or herself without a job. To go through a career without having been made redundant seems to be an exceptional feat, these days.

The people left behind are also under stress.

Another problem that is very real, but which is given far less publicity, is that of the employees left behind after a 'pruning down' of staff numbers. The survivors of redundancy often feel threatened, guilty and overworked, and they need special handling.

51

If you have ever found yourself in the position of supervising a team following a spate of redundancies, you will know the importance of:

■ building team cohesion and morale back up;
■ returning work routines to normal as soon as possible;
■ watching out for signs of stress;
■ pacing the workload, so that the new team can quickly recover their sense of pride and achievement, and not become overwhelmed by the backlog piling up.

In the period immediately following the redundancies, it may be good policy to step up the rate of work, to get over the 'change crisis'. You may find that the team members feel the need to do more to help them get over their sense of guilt. However, it is usually a mistake to make that the norm.

The next subject is very relevant to this one.

7 The right atmosphere

If you've worked in more than one organization or group, you may have detected a difference in atmosphere or 'climate'. Some places are happy and relaxed; others are stiff and formal; still others have an atmosphere of boredom – or even despair!

Activity 37

3 mins

What are the signs which tell you about the atmosphere or climate in a place of work? Try to list **two**.

_____

_____

_____

Some ways to tell are:

■ how friendly people are;
■ how considerate and supportive managers are;
■ how much people seem to enjoy their work;
■ how open people are in communicating with one another;
■ the extent to which information is made available to people about things that affect them;
■ the degree of trust between management and staff;
■ to what extent decisions are shared.

Activity 38

2 mins

Would you expect that changes would be implemented more easily if:

a   there is a friendly climate? ☐

b   managers mostly work behind closed doors? ☐

c   a number of people are complaining about the way things are at present? ☐

d   a high level of conflict exists among and between workteams? ☐

e   there is openness in communication between people? ☐

f   management are considerate and supportive? ☐

g   little mutual trust seems to be evident? ☐

If you ticked the boxes for (a), (e) and (f), I would agree with you. What about the others?

Managers who work behind closed doors (b) often find themselves mistrusted by those outside, who are likely to be suspicious of management's motivations for instigating change.

As for (c), you may argue that people who complain about the present state of affairs will be only too happy to ensure that there are no obstacles placed in the way of change. However, the complaining may be a symptom of general dissatisfaction within the organization. Change may well be needed, but it could have a stormy passage!

Where there is a high level of conflict among and between workteams (d), co-operation is usually lacking, a state of affairs that tends to be a barrier to change.

The absence of mutual trust (g) also inhibits co-operation.

We can say that:

an open, sharing, supportive, trusting and friendly atmosphere will go a long way to make the implementation of changes easier.

Suppose, in the light of what we've just said, you decide you need to bring about a change of climate in your workplace. You want to make it more responsive to changes that you know are forthcoming.

Activity 39

How long do you think it would take to bring about a change to a more open, sharing and supportive climate?

Tick whichever you think is appropriate:

I day	☐
I week	☐
2 weeks	☐
6 weeks	☐
6 months	☐
I year	☐
Longer than a year	☐

In a way, any of these suggestions could be right. However, it's very optimistic to think a great change on your part would cause more than mild surprise the next day. Perhaps if you really work at it, you'd begin to see a gradual difference in a week or two . . . or three.

Generally though, to bring about a real change in the way that people think, feel and behave towards each other takes a long time, and has to be nurtured and maintained throughout. So, to that extent, you'd be right if you thought it would take a year or longer.

Atmosphere or climate is a result of the combined attitudes and actions of everyone in the organization, and can take a lot of shifting.

The team leader may have only a limited influence over the atmosphere of the wider organization. But he or she certainly carries a lot of weight when it comes to what goes on in the workteam, and the relationships with other workteams.

In this workbook we've discussed change as a problem, a challenge and something which triggers new opportunities. It is usually all of these things. How well you, as a team leader, accommodate change depends on how well you run your team and the kind of atmosphere you are able to encourage.

A team working in a good atmosphere will generally take change in its stride.

Self-assessment 3

10 mins

For questions 1 to 6, complete the following sentences with a suitable word or words selected from the list below.

1   Where change is concerned, _____ is the best antidote to resistance.

2   _____ is the best medicine for uncertainty.

3   _____ is infectious.

4   Getting the _____ right is more than half the battle.

5   Be prepared to _____ your plans for change.

6   An open, _____, _____, trusting and _____ atmosphere will go a long way to make the implementation of changes easier.

ABANDON	INFORMATION	PRECISION
CHANGE	OPEN	SHARING
ENTHUSIASM	PARTICIPATION	SUPPORTIVE
FRIENDLY	PLANNING	UNDIVIDED

7   Which of the following statements is good advice to the team leader involved in change implementation?

   a Get the team involved in the planning process.
   b Treat change like any other routine work.
   c Before you start, plan what you want to achieve.
   d If things start to go wrong, keep it to yourself.
   e Keep everyone informed.
   f Empower your team to cope.
   g If necessary, abandon all other work while the change is going on: you can't be expected to do everything.

8   Which of the following points are the **most** important ones to be considered when planning change?

   a Training requirements.
   b Who instigated the change.
   c Changes in communication procedures.
   d How each individual will be affected.
   e The negative aspects of the change.
   f Which other groups will be affected.
   g Keeping the plans to yourself.
   h How information about the change will be issued.
   i The likely reactions and sources of resistance to the change.
   j The timetable for introducing the change.

Answers to these questions can be found on page 70.

8 Summary

- The primary skill of leading and managing is to find ways of gaining:

  - influence
  - trust and respect
  - voluntary co-operation
  - commitment to the task.

- Important aspects to the team leader's role in change include:

  - instigating change;
  - feeding information back;
  - deciding the best way to keep the team informed;
  - 'selling' the idea of the change to the team;
  - enabling the team to cope with the change;
  - providing your team with the feeling of ownership of the change;
  - coping with keeping things running during the change.

- The PIE recipe for overcoming resistance to change is:

  Participation
  Information
  Enthusiasm

- **Planning** for change involves:

  - setting objectives deciding what you want to achieve and by when;
  - identifying the key factors in the situation;
  - making a list of actions to be taken.

- In adapting to change, people may need:

  - changes of attitude
  - changes of skill
  - changes of knowledge.

- **Unfreezing** means preparing people for change.

- **Refreezing** occurs once the change has taken place: people become familiar with the new ways and learn to feel confident in them.

Performance checks

1 Quick quiz

Jot down the answers to the following questions on *Leading Change*.

Question 1 Name the **three** kinds of forces for change, which we discussed in the workbook.

_____

_____

_____

Question 2 Which **one** of the three forces for change tends to be present, with or without the other two?

_____

Question 3 What, in a word, is 'continuous, complex, untried and often difficult to manage'?

_____

Question 4 Give **two** examples of the economic pressures that organizations are frequently under. (For example, there is often pressure from workers for higher wages, shorter working hours or better conditions.)

_____

_____

Question 5 If you were asked to summarize the 'normal' or typical reaction to an unexpected job change, what would you say?

_____

_____

_____

Question 6 Briefly, how would you instil a feeling of ownership for planned change in a workteam?

_____

_____

_____

Question 7   We talked about a 'PIE recipe' for overcoming resistance to change. What do these letters stand for?

_____

Question 8   List **three** positive aspects to change.

_____

_____

_____

Question 9   We discussed the team leader's overall role in change. Name **three** of the points mentioned.

_____

_____

_____

Question 10   What is 'the best medicine for uncertainty'?

_____

Question 11   Write down the **three** main aspects of planning for change.

_____

_____

_____

Question 12   Explain briefly why 'selling' the idea of a change to the team is important.

_____

_____

_____

Question 13   What is meant by 'unfreezing' and 'refreezing' in connection with change?

_____

_____

_____

Question 14   When you start to work in a new company or department, what are the signs that tell you what the atmosphere is like?

_____

_____

_____

Question 15   'Time will generally get people used to the idea of change, and make them accept it even if they don't like it.' To what extent is this true?

_____

_____

_____

Answers to these questions can be found on page 71.

2 Workbook assessment

60 mins

Assume that, owing to reorganization and redundancies, two workteams are to be merged into one. Imagine that you previously were in charge of a workteam of ten people; now four of your original team have gone and you will take over what's left of another team – another five people. The leader of the other team has been demoted in the reshuffle, and is now working in another section. She was not very competent (in your view) but was well liked by her team members.

The new members will have to move to your part of the building and do slightly different jobs, and some retraining will be involved.

You get over the business of redundancy interviews, and you are not feeling very cheerful. Nevertheless, life (and work) must go on. In the short period before the formation of the new team, you have to draw up a plan of action.

Write down:

- what you consider your main difficulties will be;
- what your actions and priorities will be over the next days and weeks;
- how you intend to organize things.

Then write a paragraph explaining your overall approach.

Make any assumptions you wish about the kind of work that the company does, and the kind of retraining that will be needed. If you wish you can base any details not defined above on your own job, or one that you have done in the past.

Your complete answer to this assessment need not be longer than a single page.

3 Work-based assignment

60 mins

The time guide for this assignment gives you an approximate idea of how long it is likely to take you to write up your findings. You will find you need to spend some additional time gathering information, perhaps talking to colleagues and thinking about the assignment.

This assignment may provide the basis of appropriate evidence for your S/NVQ portfolio. The Assignment is designed to help you to demonstrate:

- what you would do or would have done to obtain the commitment of others;
- your ability to analyse and conceptualize, by showing that you can think clearly and objectively about the past, and to apply your thinking to present and future plans;
- your teambuilding skills;
- your ability to focus on results;
- your ability to take decisions;
- your ability to influence others.

What you have to do

For this Assignment, you are asked to describe a major change that you have managed with a workteam in the past, and to explain it and comment on it, in the light of what you have read in this workbook.

Possible events are:

- a restructuring, in which some people were promoted, others taking on new roles etc.;
- moving premises;
- a new product or service being introduced;
- a merger or take-over which affected your team.

If your work experience is limited, and you have had no participation in managing during a period of significant change, you could instead describe and investigate a change that affected others. (However, this option may be less useful in terms of your portfolio of evidence.)

In either case, you will need to identify **three** people who were affected by the change, and to interview them, in order to find out more about the implementation of the change, and how these individuals reacted to it.

Get answers to the following questions:

- How was the change announced?
- How were you and others affected by it?
- What was your and their initial response when the news first broke?
- How did you, individually and collectively, manage to adapt to the change?
- What, in the light of subsequent events, would you have done differently, or would have had others do differently.

There may also be documents that you can refer to which give some background to the change.

You should record your findings, and then try to decide what can be deduced from the information you have gleaned. Your overall aim in this assignment is to answer the following questions.

■ What have I discovered about how the team felt about and reacted to this event, in terms of the features and process of change described in this workbook?

■ How will this knowledge help me to lead change more effectively in the future?

For example:

■ If you noted resistance to the change, what grounds were given for this resistance? Was it justified in terms of the perceived benefits and drawbacks, or was the resistance simply a normal human reaction to any kind of change?

■ Do you think the organization's 'climate' at the time was conducive to change implementation?

■ What was communication like – good or poor? Were you and other managers kept well-informed? To what extent do you think you were successful in informing team members of the purpose and intention of the change, and of persuading them of its value?

■ Most important of all: what, in your opinion, should have been done differently? (Be as precise as possible in your answer to this question.)

What you should write

1 Write down your findings regarding the past change, either in the form of a report, or as a memo addressed to your line manager.

2 Add to your report or memo a list of key pointers, which are relevant to the next change on your work horizon.

The whole document does not have to be more than two or three pages long.

Reflect and review

1 Reflect and review

Now that you have completed your work on *Leading Change*, let us review our workbook objectives. First:

You should be better able to identify the forces behind change, and be aware of forthcoming changes.

We reviewed three major forces behind change of all kinds: economics, technology and social or legal factors. Economics, inevitably, figures largely in most plans for change. Technology, too, drives change along at a relentless pace, and few organizations can afford to allow themselves to remain ignorant of the potential benefits that it can bring. As to social aspects, we have noted the fact that the tide of public opinion can force governments and companies large and small to rethink their policies.

It is useful for you as a team leader to identify which one or more of these factors is in operation when a change occurs. What is of even more value is to make yourself aware of known developments before you get overtaken by events.

You may want to ask yourself the following questions regarding these points.

■ To what extent do I spend time considering the causes of change in my work?

_____

_____

_____

■ How could I find out more about events which may result in changes in my job and my organization in the future?

_____

_____

_____

The second workbook objective was as follows:

You should be better able to anticipate and recognize reactions to change, and overcome resistance to change.

Reactions, as we have seen, will depend very much on:

- the way that a change is presented;
- how well the team leader or manager is able to 'sell' the idea of the change;
- the extent to which the operation is carefully planned;
- how much thought is given to the manner in which information is released.

Some questions you may like to ask yourself are:

- What could I do to improve my ability to recognize and anticipate reactions among my team?

  _____

  _____

  _____

- How could my methods of communicating with the team regarding management plans be improved?

  _____

  _____

  _____

- How might I approach the question of 'selling' new ideas in a more productive way?

  _____

  _____

  _____

The next workbook objective was:

You should be better able to recognize the beneficial aspects of change, and adopt a positive attitude towards new thinking.

We have agreed that not all change is welcome (especially when you are suffering from 'change fatigue'), but that there is usually an 'up' and a 'down' side to every set of plans. Any particular change is liable to be seen as either completely desirable or totally unattractive: it often takes some thought to identify the other side of the coin.

If disadvantages are not recognized, they may present unexpected snags, but there are usually ways around every problem.

However, by learning to recognize the good points of a proposed change, which may include:

- bringing **new interest** to the job;
- opening up new prospects for **career development**;
- showing a **new slant on things**;
- providing the opportunity to learn **new skills**;
- posing a **challenge**;
- giving greater **empowerment** to the team;

you stand to benefit most from it.

Some questions which you may feel to be appropriate when considering the implications of a proposal are:

- How can I and my team members get the most from this change?

  _____

  _____

  _____

- In what ways can the change be used as a step towards new career developments for each of us?

  _____

  _____

  _____

- How can we meet the challenge of this change and find new interest in the work through it?

  _____

  _____

  _____

- What is good about this change?

  _____

  _____

  _____

Our final objective was:

You should be better able to manage the implementation of change, in particular by aiming to give your team a sense of ownership of the plans they are to implement, and so win their commitment.

Here is the central 'message' of the workbook: that change has to be 'sold' to the team, so that they can become its proprietors, its defenders and the champions of change.

I suggested the PIE recipe: participation, information and enthusiasm, as vital ingredients of this key strategy. Ideally, the team should feel that the change plans are in their charge; it may certainly be the case that the change won't be successfully implemented without their full commitment to it.

Your questions for this objective could include:

- What steps will I need to take during the management of this change? (Use the two checklists on pages 46, and 47.)

- How can I persuade my team (the potential buyers) that they will benefit from taking ownership of the change, in exchange for their pledge to the cause?

---

2 Action plan

> **EXTENSION 2**
> The book in our extension takes a slightly different approach in its Chapter 11, 'Winning at change — a personal action plan'. It's worth reading, if you have time.

Use this plan to further develop for yourself a course of action you want to take. Make a note in the left-hand column of the issues or problems you want to tackle, and then decide what you intend to do, and make a note in Column 2.

The resources you need might include time, materials, information or money. You may need to negotiate for some of them, but they could be something easily acquired, like half an hour of somebody's time, or a chapter of a book. Put whatever you need in Column 3. No plan means anything without a timescale, so put a realistic target completion date in Column 4.

Finally, describe the outcome you want to achieve as a result of this plan, whether it is for your own benefit or advancement, or a more efficient way of doing things.

Desired outcomes

1 Issues	2 Action	3 Resources	4 Target completion

Actual outcomes

3 Extensions

Extension 1

Book   *Organizational Behaviour*
Authors   Andrzej Huczynski and David Buchanan
Edition   Second edition 1991
Publisher   Prentice Hall International

This is a useful book about management and organizations generally, and is not difficult to read. Chapter 20: 'Managing change' is particularly relevant to our subject. This chapter introduces the following twelve concepts:

- Levels of change
- Adhocracy
- Future shock
- Internal triggers of change
- External triggers of change
- Proactive change

- The entrepreneurial spirit
- Self-fulfilling prophecy
- Self-defeating prophecy
- Alternative futures
- Resistance to change
- The British disease

Extension 2

Book   *Winning at Change*
Authors   George Blair and Sandy Meadows
Edition   1996
Publisher   Pitman

As the authors say in the foreword: 'We have designed this book to help busy managers like you across all sectors not only to survive, but win at organizational change.' There are 201 pages, written in an easy-to-read style.

The chapter headings are: 1 Why change won't go away; 2 Can you manage in the whirlpool?; 3 Can you meet the challenge?; 4 Assessing yourself; 5 Tailoring change to your organization; 6 Empowerment; 7 TQM; 8 Re-engineering; 9 Skills for mastering change; 10 Influencing the direction of change; 11 Winning at change – a personal action plan; 12 What if you want to choose to bail out?

Extension 3

Book   *Managing Change*
Author   Philip Sadler
Edition   1995
Publisher   Kogan Page (*The Sunday Times* Business Skills Series)

This is another useful and interesting book devoted to the subject of change management. If you do not have time to read the whole book, three chapters are of particular relevance: 3 The nature of organizational change; 8 Making it happen – the process of implementation; 9 Case studies.

These Extensions can be taken up via your NEBS Management Centre. They will either have them or will arrange that you have access to them. However, it may be more convenient to check out the materials with your personnel or training people at work – they may well give you access. There are other good reasons for approaching your own people; for example, they will become aware of your interest and you can involve them in your development.

4 Answers to Self-assessment questions

Self-assessment 1 on page 17

1 Changes come about because of TECHNOLOGY, social or legal factors and, more often than not, ECONOMICS.

2 Wise managers make it their business to keep a close watch on CHANGING events in their own INDUSTRY, whatever the causes.

3 In a very real sense, CHANGE *is* the norm.

4 All organizations have to be FLEXIBLE enough to respond to change quickly.

5 OWNERSHIP is the key to success in implementing change.

6 The successful organizations ensure that everyone:

a gets the chance to PARTICIPATE in realizing the change
b has the right INFORMATION, knowledge and SKILLS to handle the change.

7 The companies which adapt to a changing environment most successfully will, among other things:

c provide variety and flexibility in jobs and keep everyone informed of what's going on;

Reasons: The company in (a) does not exhibit flexibility; (b) does not allow people enough participation in the decisions; (d) tries to restrict knowledge and understanding. (c) avoids these pitfalls.

Self-assessment 2 on page 29

1 The answer is as follows.

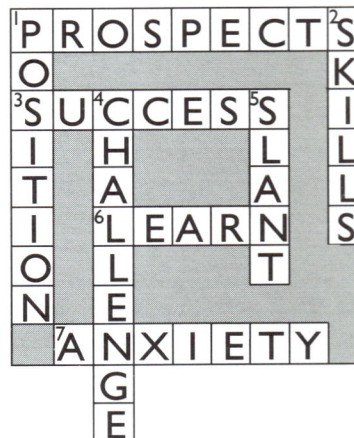

2 Resistance to change is NORMAL.

3 Emotional outbursts are often triggered by UNCERTAINTY ABOUT CHANGE.

4 One of the positive aspects of change is that it CAN PROVIDE A NEW CHALLENGE.

5 Work is more rewarding for those who learn to identify the POSITIVE ASPECTS OF CHANGE.

Self-assessment 3 on page 55

1 Where change is concerned, PARTICIPATION is the best antidote to resistance.

2 INFORMATION is the best medicine for uncertainty.

3 ENTHUSIASM is infectious.

4 Getting the PLANNING right is more than half the battle.

5 Be prepared to CHANGE your plans for change.

6 An open, SHARING, SUPPORTIVE, trusting and FRIENDLY atmosphere will go a long way to make the implementation of changes easier.

7 (a), (c), (e), and (f) are good advice.

8 (a), (c), (d), (f), (h), (i) and (j) are the most important aspects to be considered when planning change.

5 Answers to the quick quiz

Answer 1   The three forces are: technological, social or legal, and economic.

Answer 2   Economics tends to be behind many changes, even when technology, social or legal factors, is also acting as a force for change.

Answer 3   Change!

Answer 4   Organizations are frequently under the pressure of competition: pressure from shareholders; pressure from financial institutions; pressure from employees.

Answer 5   The only sensible answer is that there is no typical reaction: people react in different ways to different situations. However, it can be said to be quite 'normal' for change to be received with suspicion or hostility.

Answer 6   There are many possible answers to this question. One was summed up on page 16 as follows: The successful organizations ensure that everyone:

■ gets the chance to participate in realizing the change;
■ has the right information, knowledge and skills to handle the change.

Answer 7   Participation, Information, Enthusiasm.

Answer 8   There are many positive aspects. We mentioned that change may:

■ bring **new interest** to the job;
■ open up new prospects for **career development**;
■ show a **new slant on things**;
■ provide the opportunity to learn **new skills**;
■ pose a **challenge;**
■ give greater **empowerment** to the team;

Answer 9   The aspects to the team leader's role in change we mentioned were: instigating change; being aware of potential changes; calculating costs; determining feasibility; feeding information back; working out a strategy for deployment of staff; deciding the best way to keep the team informed; 'selling' the idea of the change to the team; enabling the team to cope with the change; providing your team with the feeling of ownership of the change; planning the logistics; coping with keeping things running during the change.

Answer 10   Information is the best medicine for uncertainty.

Answer 11   In general, the process of planning consists of:

■ deciding what you want to achieve and by when – the objectives of the plan;
■ identifying the key factors in the situation;
■ making a list of actions to be taken.

71

Answer 12   'Selling' the idea of change means persuading the team to take ownership of it, in exchange for their commitment. It is important because, until and unless the team is 'sold on the idea' you will have difficulty in getting their full co-operation.

Answer 13   Unfreezing means reducing resistance towards change and creating a climate in which change can take place more easily. Refreezing is a word for the process whereby people become familiar with the new ideas and new ways, and feel confident with them.

Answer 14   The signs include how friendly people are; how supportive managers and team leaders are; how open people are in communicating with each other; the degree of trust that exists; to what extent decisions are shared.

Answer 15   I would say that time does cure all ills – eventually. But time may not make people start liking something, if they disagree with it.

6 Certificate

Completion of this certificate by an authorized person shows that you have worked through all the parts of this workbook and satisfactorily completed the assessments. The certificate provides a record of what you have done that may be used for exemptions or as evidence of prior learning against other nationally certificated qualifications.

Pergamon Flexible Learning and NEBS Management are always keen to refine and improve their products. One of the key sources of information to help this process are people who have just used the product. If you have any information or views, good or bad, please pass them on.

NEBS
MANAGEMENT
DEVELOPMENT

SUPER SERIES

THIRD EDITION

Leading Change

....

has satisfactorily completed this workbook

Name of signatory ....

Position ....

Signature ....

Date ....

Official stamp

SUPER SERIES

SUPER SERIES 3

0-7506-3362-X   Full Set of Workbooks, User Guide and Support Guide

A. Managing Activities

0-7506-3295-X	1. Planning and Controlling Work
0-7506-3296-8	2. Understanding Quality
0-7506-3297-6	3. Achieving Quality
0-7506-3298-4	4. Caring for the Customer
0-7506-3299-2	5. Marketing and Selling
0-7506-3300-X	6. Managing a Safe Environment
0-7506-3301-8	7. Managing Lawfully - Health, Safety and Environment
0-7506-37064	8. Preventing Accidents
0-7506-3302-6	9. Leading Change
0-7506-4091-X	10. Auditing Quality

B. Managing Resources

0-7506-3303-4	1. Controlling Physical Resources
0-7506-3304-2	2. Improving Efficiency
0-7506-3305-0	3. Understanding Finance
0-7506-3306-9	4. Working with Budgets
0-7506-3307-7	5. Controlling Costs
0-7506-3308-5	6. Making a Financial Case
0-7506-4092-8	7. Managing Energy Efficiency

C. Managing People

0-7506-3309-3	1. How Organisations Work
0-7506-3310-7	2. Managing with Authority
0-7506-3311-5	3. Leading Your Team
0-7506-3312-3	4. Delegating Effectively
0-7506-3313-1	5. Working in Teams
0-7506-3314-X	6. Motivating People
0-7506-3315-8	7. Securing the Right People
0-7506-3316-6	8. Appraising Performance
0-7506-3317-4	9. Planning Training and Development
0-75063318-2	10. Delivering Training
0-7506-3320-4	11. Managing Lawfully - People and Employment
0-7506-3321-2	12. Commitment to Equality
0-7506-3322-0	13. Becoming More Effective
0-7506-3323-9	14. Managing Tough Times
0-7506-3324-7	15. Managing Time

D. Managing Information

0-7506-3325-5	1. Collecting Information
0-7506-3326-3	2. Storing and Retrieving Information
0-7506-3327-1	3. Information in Management
0-7506-3328-X	4. Communication in Management
0-7506-3329-8	5. Listening and Speaking
0-7506-3330-1	6. Communicating in Groups
0-7506-3331-X	7. Writing Effectively
0-7506-3332-8	8. Project and Report Writing
0-7506-3333-6	9. Making and Taking Decisions
0-7506-3334-4	10. Solving Problems

SUPER SERIES 3 USER GUIDE + SUPPORT GUIDE

0-7506-37056	1. User Guide
0-7506-37048	2. Support Guide

SUPER SERIES 3 CASSETTE TITLES

0-7506-3707-2	1. Complete Cassette Pack
0-7506-3711-0	2. Reaching Decisions
0-7506-3712-9	3. Making a Financial Case
0-7506-3710-2	4. Customers Count
0-7506-3709-9	5. Being the Best
0-7506-3708-0	6. Working Together

To Order - phone us direct for prices and availability details
(please quote ISBNs when ordering)
College orders: 01865 314333 • Account holders: 01865 314301
Individual purchases: 01865 314627 (please have credit card details ready)

We Need Your Views

We really need your views in order to make the Super Series 3 (SS3) an even better learning tool for you. Please take time out to complete and return this questionnaire to Management Marketing Department, Pergamon Flexible Learning, Linacre House, Jordan Hill, Oxford, OX2 8DP.

Name:...

Address:..

....

Title of workbook:..

If applicable, please state which qualification you are studying for. If not, please describe what study you are undertaking, and with which organisation or college:

....

Please grade the following out of 10 (10 being extremely good, 0 being extremely poor):

Content   ....   Appropriateness to your position   ....

Readability   ....   Qualification coverage   ....

What did you particularly like about this workbook?

....
....
....

Are there any features you disliked about this workbook? Please identify them.

....
....
....

Are there any errors we have missed? If so, please state page number: ....

How are you using the material? For example, as an open learning course, as a reference resource, as a training resource etc.

....

How did you hear about Super Series 3?:

Word of mouth: ☐   Through my tutor/trainer: ☐   Mailshot: ☐

Other (please give details):..

....

Many thanks for your help in returning this form.